RISE!

FROM CAGED BIRD TO POET OF THE PEOPLE, Maya Angelou

by BETHANY HEGEDUS · foreword by COLIN JOHNSON · illustrations by TONYA ENGEL

Lee & Low Books Inc.
NEW YORK

TO SUSAN, AND ALL SURVIVORS. TO THE LIFE AND LEGACY OF
MAYA ANGELOU, WHOSE WISDOM AND WIT TAUGHT ME TO EMBRACE
THE HEALING POWER OF THE WRITTEN AND SPOKEN WORD. —B.H.

TO ZOË—YOU ARE MY MOON, THE SWEETEST LITTLE STAR, AND THE
BEST THING THAT'S EVER HAPPENED TO ME. I LOVE YOU! —T.E.

Acknowledgments

This book would not exist without the time and talents of so many: Alexandra Penfold, who believed from the beginning. Jessica Echeverria, who climbed into the editorial trenches with me. Dr. Ebony Elizabeth Thomas, for her insight that was both a beacon and an opportunity. Jennifer Lash at CMG Worldwide. Colin Johnson and The Caged Bird Legacy for trusting us to rise to the occasion as we depicted the life and legacy of one of America's finest talents. A big thank-you to all the hands and hearts of the Lee & Low team who have touched this piece while it became a book, and most especially to Tonya Engel, whose passion and pure poetry in the visual medium gave the text the ability to soar. —B.H.

Text copyright © 2019 by Bethany Hegedus
Foreword copyright © 2019 by Colin Johnson
Illustrations copyright © 2019 by Tonya Engel
All rights reserved. No part of this book may be reproduced, transmitted, or stored in an information retrieval system in any form or by any means, electronic, mechanical, photocopying, recording, or otherwise, without written permission from the publisher.
LEE & LOW BOOKS Inc., 95 Madison Avenue, New York, NY 10016
leeandlow.com
Edited by Jessica V. Echeverria
Designed by Liz Casal
Production by The Kids at Our House
The text is set in Avenir and Avallon
The illustrations are rendered in acrylic underpainting and oils on textured mono-printed papers.
Manufactured in China by Toppan
Printed on paper from responsible sources
10 9 8 7 6 5 4 3 2 1
First Edition

Library of Congress Cataloging-in-Publication Data
Names: Hegedus, Bethany, author. | Johnson, Colin (Colin Ashanti), writer of foreword. | Engel, Tonya, illustrator.
Title: Rise: from caged bird to poet of the people, Maya Angelou / by Bethany Hegedus;
foreword by Colin Johnson; illustrations by Tonya Engel.
Description: First edition. | New York, NY: Lee & Low Books Inc., [2019]
Audience: Ages 7-10. | Audience: Grades 4-6. | Includes bibliographical references.
Identifiers: LCCN 2018047660 | ISBN 9781620145876 (hardcover: alk. paper)
Subjects: LCSH: Angelou, Maya–Juvenile literature. | African American women authors–20th century–Biography.
Classification: LCC PS3551.N464 Z6934 2019 | DDC 818/.5409–dc23
LC record available at https://lccn.loc.gov/2018047660

Foreword

As a young girl, my grandmother Marguerite Johnson—better known as Maya Angelou—was raised by young parents who had difficult childhoods of their own. Vivian Baxter and Bailey Johnson didn't really know what to do with small children. Add to that discord a racial climate in America that found many African Americans using desperate measures to survive. Despite a tough life, my grandmother became courageous and compassionate, developing a great empathy for children and their journey through childhood.

Childhood is often a time when the power in life belongs to the adults around you. Empathizing with the innocence of children, my grandmother believed they deserved a good start in life but also possessed the courage to endure and thrive no matter their circumstances. The love of Grandmother Henderson, Uncle Willie, her brother, Bailey, and Mrs. Flowers helped her to grow in courage, while reading helped her understand the unlimited possibilities of life. She would later write, "Courage is the most important of all the virtues because without courage you cannot practice any other virtue consistently."

My grandmother believed that courage started with the simplicity of realizing that there are no monsters under the bed. Or, if you do have human monsters to overcome, courage was an inner virtue that could be developed early. As she moved past the pains of her own childhood and managed that pain, she came to believe: "My mission in life is not merely to survive, but to thrive; and to do so with some passion, some compassion, some humor, and some style."

As you read this book with your children, I hope they will ask questions and make comments; and as you listen deeply, I hope your conversations will help them build courage that will serve them throughout their lives.

—Colin Johnson

The train looms,
   a mass of metal
   and steel.
Maya and her brother, Bailey,
   hold hands.
Like luggage they have been packed
   and shipped off
   to Stamps, Arkansas.
Their bellies rumble;
   strangers feed them
   cold ham and a biscuit.
Bailey, a year older, offers
   Maya comfort.
His voice a lullaby,
   his skin a warm blanket,
   his smile rocks and reassures.
The train chugs south;
   the future is yet to be.

In Stamps,
Momma Henderson—
  as tall as a Sycamore,
  as dignified as a Queen—
  rules the roost.
She owns the William Johnson General Store.
  She owns!
And has owned for twenty-five years.
Maya's Uncle Willie—
  wearing a starched shirt and shined shoes—
  eagerly awaits the new arrivals.
The family store stands before Maya,
  an unopened present,
  the front door a ribbon
    waiting to be pulled.

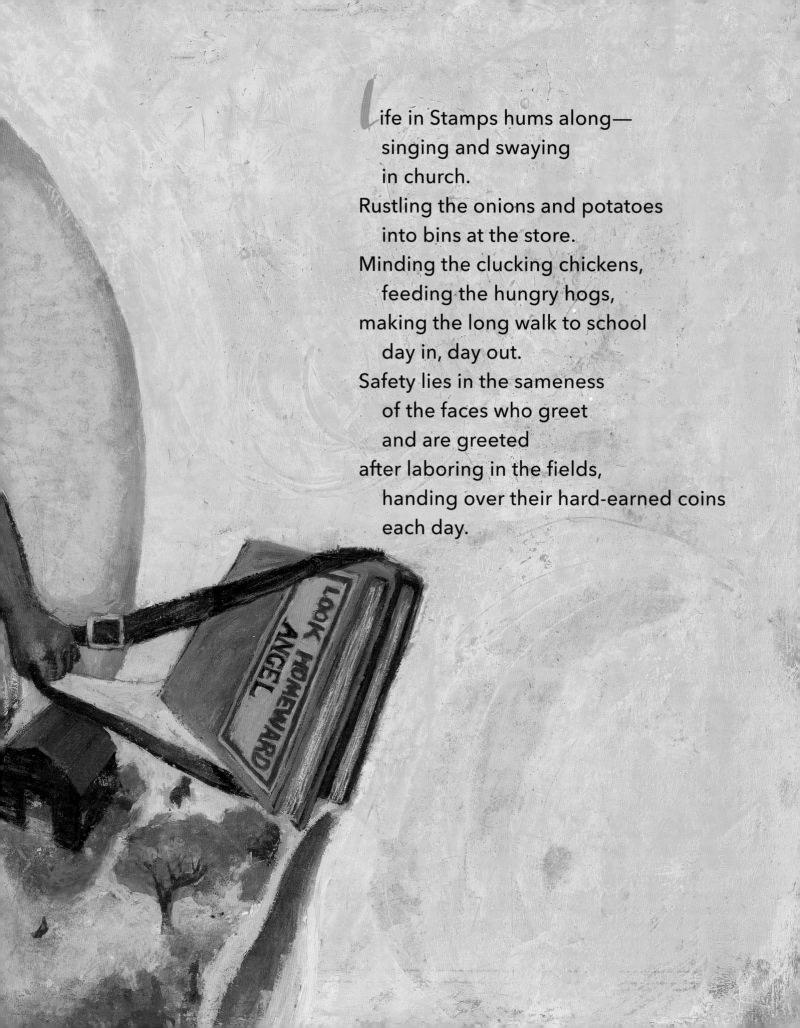

Life in Stamps hums along—
singing and swaying
in church.
Rustling the onions and potatoes
into bins at the store.
Minding the clucking chickens,
feeding the hungry hogs,
making the long walk to school
day in, day out.
Safety lies in the sameness
of the faces who greet
and are greeted
after laboring in the fields,
handing over their hard-earned coins
each day.

It doesn't take long before white girls,
　　not much older than Maya,
　　enter the store, wielding their whiteness
　　as a weapon, a sword
　　meant to cut the giant Sycamore.
They call Momma Henderson "Annie."
　　Not "missus."
　　Not "ma'am."
　　Just *Annie.*
Maya curls her hands
　　into fists
　　that stay rooted
　　at her sides.
She watches as Queen Henderson, proud
　　but not defiant,
　　answers.
The scales of justice
　　are stacked against them.
Young Maya
　　loves Stamps.
Young Maya
　　hates Stamps.
　　　　Hate and love,
love and hate:
the seesaw of the South.

Maya is six
   when Mother sends for them.
Overnight, Maya and Bailey are shipped off
   again.
Unlike Stamps, St. Louis is fast—
   full of juke joints,
   numbers runners,
   and card games.
Mother Vivian is a beauty,
   regal with red lips.
Maya, always told she's plain,
   and not as pretty as her mother
   or as handsome as Bailey,
feels discarded
   amid the hustle.
Mother's attention is split even more
when Mr. Freeman, her boyfriend, comes calling.

One day, Maya, left alone
with Mr. Freeman,
is anything but free.
After a visit to the hospital,
Maya calls out Mr. Freeman's name
as the one
who hurt her.
Mr. Freeman spends only one night
in jail.
Later, he is found crumpled
behind the slaughterhouse.
Maya falls silent,
scared her voice
struck him
dead.

Maya and Bailey are returned
to the strong limbs
of Momma Henderson.
Life in Stamps continues—
onions and potatoes,
chickens and hogs.
But for Maya there is
no laughing,
no humming,
no music.
Her heart aches to survive;
her mind whispers to itself
as she reads and reads and reads.
Books offer solace.
Books offer safety.

The floorboards
of Momma Henderson's store creak.
Mrs. Flowers, the Lady of Stamps,
    smelling of talcum,
    dressed in cotton chiffon,
    invites Maya to her home.
Maya steps out from behind the flour bins
    and nods her consent.
The Lady of Stamps offers Maya
    sweet lemonade, flat tea cookies,
    and a book. Dickens: *A Tale of Two Cities*.
"It was the best of times, it was the worst of times."
Maya has read these words before,
    but hearing them glide gracefully
    from Mrs. Flowers's smiling lips
    is different.
Maya awakens to the power of the spoken word.

Outside, Maya is quiet.
   Inside, words make music.
Maya memorizes the rhythm,
   sways to the exquisite dance,
      the twisting, turning
   conga line of language
that pulses across the page.
The words of others
   live inside Maya now,
though she refuses to speak
   to anyone but Bailey, her protector.
Under Momma Henderson's bed,
   under the stairs of the store,
Maya begins to read
   aloud.
Slowly, Maya rises out of her grief
   and confusion,
   and does more than answer,
   "Yes, ma'am." "No, sir."
Her words,
   her feelings,
   her voice
      welcome her home.

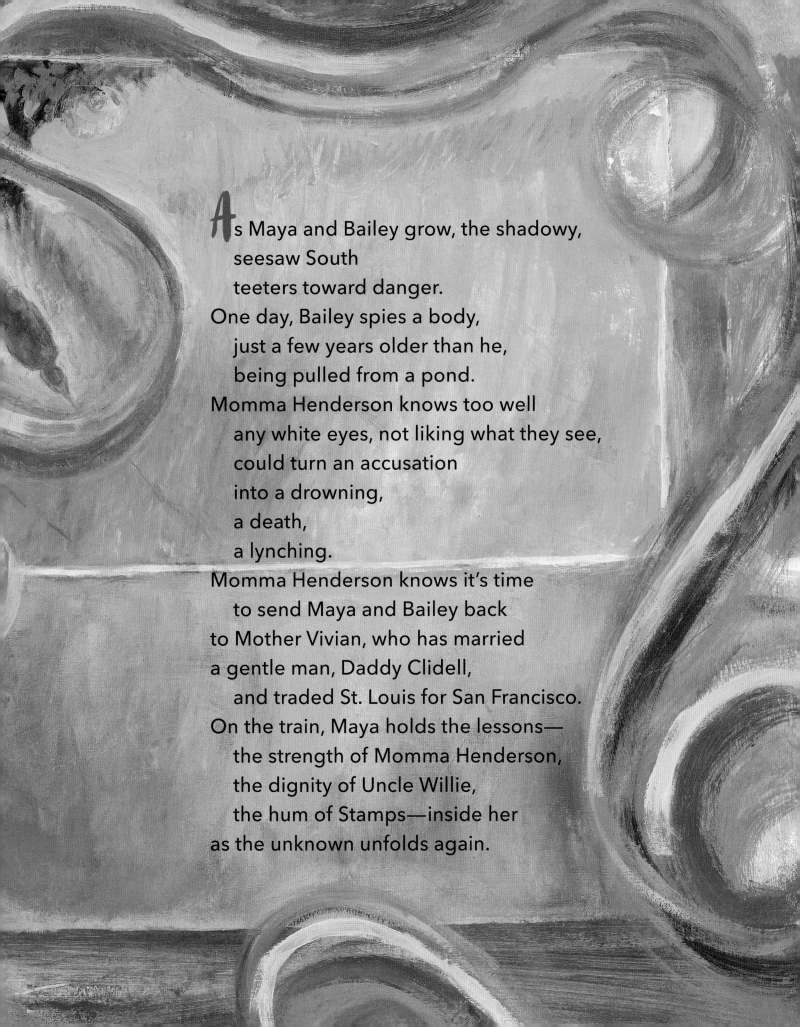

As Maya and Bailey grow, the shadowy,
    seesaw South
    teeters toward danger.
One day, Bailey spies a body,
    just a few years older than he,
    being pulled from a pond.
Momma Henderson knows too well
    any white eyes, not liking what they see,
    could turn an accusation
    into a drowning,
    a death,
    a lynching.
Momma Henderson knows it's time
    to send Maya and Bailey back
to Mother Vivian, who has married
a gentle man, Daddy Clidell,
    and traded St. Louis for San Francisco.
On the train, Maya holds the lessons—
    the strength of Momma Henderson,
    the dignity of Uncle Willie,
    the hum of Stamps—inside her
as the unknown unfolds again.

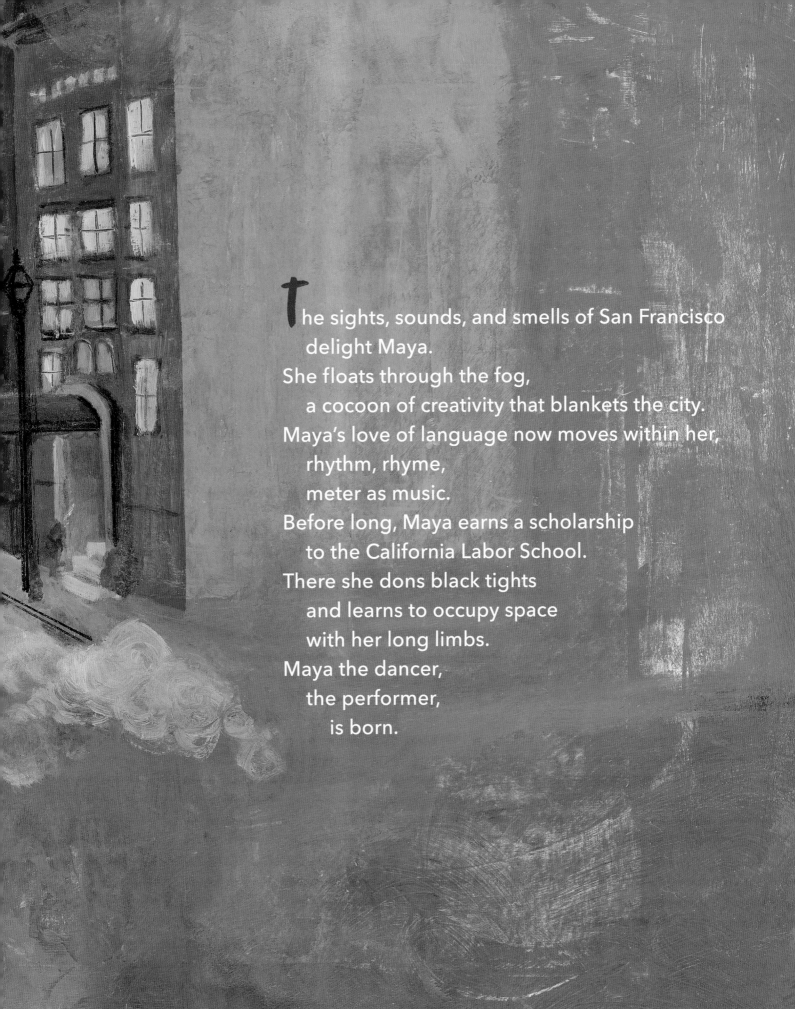

The sights, sounds, and smells of San Francisco
　　delight Maya.
She floats through the fog,
　　a cocoon of creativity that blankets the city.
Maya's love of language now moves within her,
　　rhythm, rhyme,
　　meter as music.
Before long, Maya earns a scholarship
　　to the California Labor School.
There she dons black tights
　　and learns to occupy space
　　with her long limbs.
Maya the dancer,
　　the performer,
　　　is born.

Maya's feet tap to the jitterbug.
   Her legs kick to the Lindy.
She is an entertainer.
   A trolley car conductor.
   A high school graduate.
   A young mother.
Leaving home, Maya has to work many jobs—
   flipping burgers,
   stripping paint off cars—
all to support her son, Guy.

Rising before the alarm,
Maya wonders how her passions,
   her artistry,
   can pay the bills
   and provide for her and Guy.
Eventually, she finds her way
   to the Purple Onion,
   the premiere place
   to see and be seen.
Performing takes Maya far—
   first to Milan and Venice,
   dancing and singing
   in *Porgy and Bess*.
After that to Paris, City of Lights,
   then on to Cairo,
   where faces as dark as hers
   hold positions of authority.
From city to city,
   she struts and sways.

When Maya returns to the States,
    her heart longs to stay,
    to not be away from Guy,
    to plant roots in her community,
roots that will give them both the strength to soar.
Maya joins the Harlem Writers' Circle,
    gathering with a group of writers—
    Rosa Guy, Louise Meriwether,
    Langston Hughes, and more.
Together work is read,
    strengths and weaknesses
    are shared; talent explodes.
Maya discovers a voice that is
    as gravelly and gritty,
    as jubilant and joyous
    on the page
    as it is on the stage.
Maya hears Dr. King preach from a Baptist pulpit.
    His voice rises to the rafters
    as Maya is transported back
    to the seesaw South.
Maya answers the call
    of freedom for all.
Maya the activist takes flight.
    She writes, produces, and performs,
    praising and raising funds
for civil rights.

After a threatening phone call comes,
   her safety is shattered.
Maya and her family flee to Cairo,
   where Maya the journalist is born.
In Ghana, Malcolm X,
   a fiery voice for human rights,
   has also journeyed to the motherland.
Maya and other Americans flock to meet him.
Taking note of her passion and compassion,
   Malcolm invites Maya
   to work at his new center in the States.
Guy, almost full grown,
   urges his mother to say
      yes.

Maya lands in New York ready to work.
Three days later, Malcolm falls to the floor,
    the stench of gunfire lingering
    in the crowded air.
Broken, Maya must rise,
    only to be trampled again
    when Dr. King is assassinated
    on Maya's birthday, April 4.
The day is no longer a day of celebration
    but a day of mourning,
    a howling at the injustices of the world,
    at the dangerous seesaw
    that cuts off the lives of those
    who dare to dream.
James Baldwin—poet, novelist, friend—
    urges Maya not to retreat
    but to unlock the pain, to free it
    once and for all.
Maya vows not to go mute.
    There is no safety in silence.

Delving deep into her past,
Maya begins a memoir,
    circling the scars
    of the caged bird.
She raises her pen and lets her words
    her words
make music.
The sentences dive and dance;
    her life story surges and soars.
Books fly from her fingertips:
    poetry, memoirs,
    bestsellers all.
Maya, with a tilt to her head,
    a sway in her hips,
    sometimes with her own ruby-red lips,
offers up her words to the women
    who came before:
    the sturdiness of Momma Henderson,
    the beauty of Mother Vivian.
And to all the women and men
    whose bodies and souls endured
    slavery
        and abuse.

On January 20, 1993,
Maya stands before her country.
She rises up before
    the towns that were once divided,
    the doors that were once closed,
    the lives that were once lost,
and with her deep, gravelly voice
    recites a poem she wrote
        she wrote
    for the people,
    and the new president.
Hearing her words,
    the pulse of the morning
    is felt by all.
The applause,
    from black hands,
    from white hands,
    from all hands,
is as loud as a train,
    rolling and rumbling
    into the station
    proclaiming
Maya poet of the people.

At the age of eighty-six,
this phenomenal woman,
 who spent a lifetime breaking free,
 finally rests her wings.
As her heart
 beats its last beat . . .

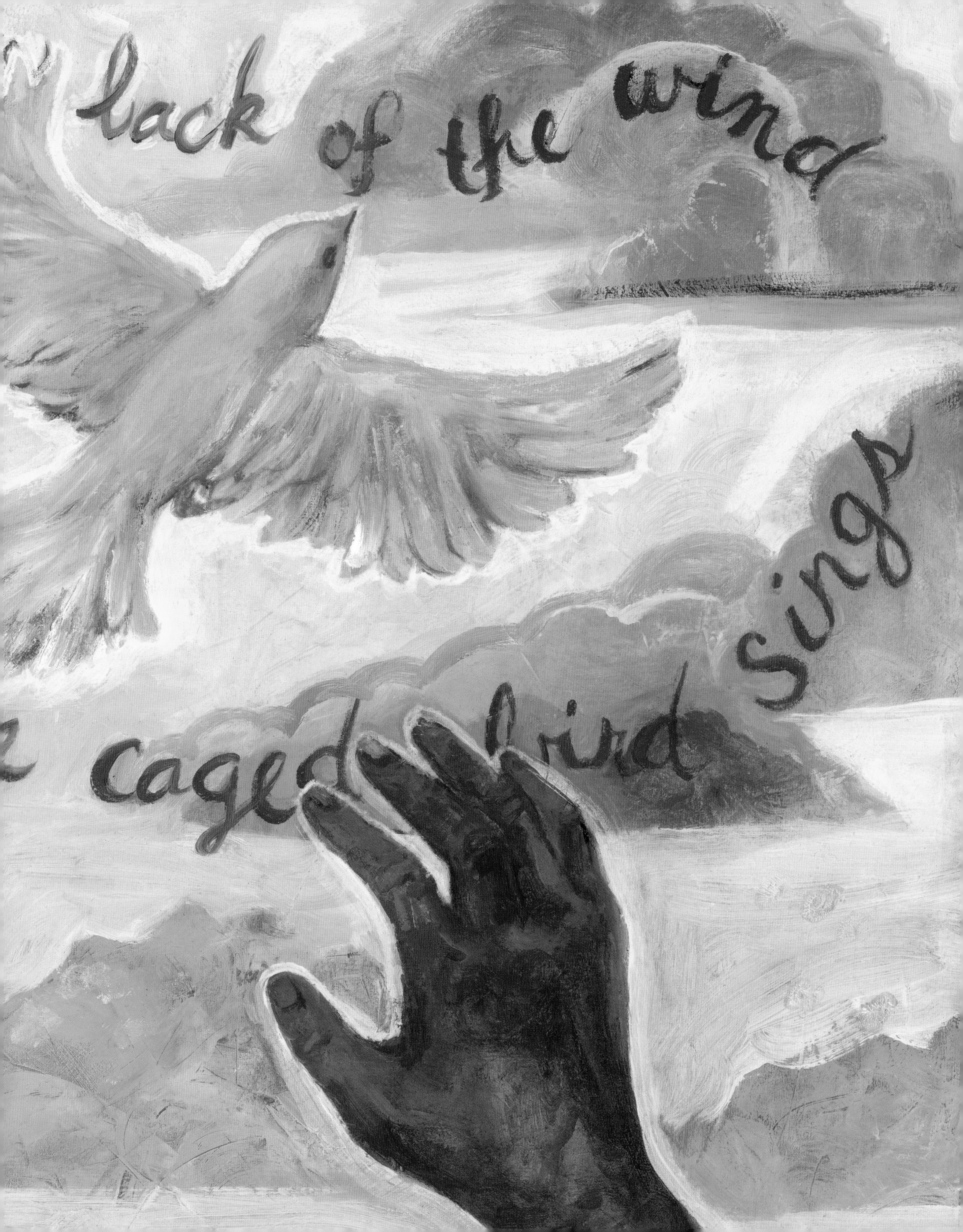
lack of the wind
caged bird sings

I Rise.
Leaving behind nights of terror and fe
Just like moons and like
with the certainty of tides
Just like hopes

. . . her words
her words
still rise.
They will always
rise
rise

rise.

Did you want to see me

broken toward

who poured ...and followed ones

Phenomenal Woman

The life of Dr. Maya Angelou was in a word . . . phenomenal.
Maya Angelou's many books and her legacy of not just surviving
but thriving continue to give us all hope to rise again and again.

**"We may encounter many defeats
but we must not be defeated."**
—Dr. Maya Angelou, 1928-2014

Maya Angelou, age 7 or 8.

*Photo: Dr. Maya Angelou used with
permission from Caged Bird Legacy, LLC*

Time Line

1928 Marguerite Annie Johnson—best known as
Maya Angelou—is born on April 4 to parents Vivian
Baxter and Bailey Johnson in St. Louis, Missouri.
Bailey Jr. is her older brother.

1931 Parents divorce. Maya and her brother, Bailey,
are sent via train to Stamps, Arkansas, to live with their
father's mother, Annie Henderson. Maya is three. A note
is pinned to each of them: "To whom it may concern, in
care of Miss Annie Henderson, Stamps, Arkansas."

1934 Maya and Bailey are taken to St. Louis to stay
with their mother. While there, Vivian's boyfriend,
Mr. Freeman, sexually abuses Maya. He is arrested
after Maya testifies. The next evening Mr. Freeman is
released and then found dead. Maya doesn't speak
for nearly six years, thinking her voice killed him.

Maya and Bailey return to Stamps, Arkansas, under
the care of Momma Henderson, their grandmother.

1939 Maya is tutored by Stamps resident Mrs.
Flowers. Maya begins to read out loud.

After years of being selectively mute, Maya

begins to speak to more people than just Bailey and occasionally Momma Henderson.

1940   Maya and Bailey move to San Francisco. Their mother has married a man they call Daddy Clidell. Maya is awarded a dance scholarship and attends the California Labor School.

1942   When Bailey drops out of school, Maya does the same and begins work as the first African American cable car conductor in San Francisco.

1944   Maya has returned to high school, and days after graduation, she gives birth to her only child, Guy Johnson.

1950   Maya performs at San Francisco's Purple Onion, a well-known club.

1952   Maya marries Tosh Angelos, a Greek sailor. She takes his last name and is now known as Maya Angelou. They divorce a few years later.

1954-1955   Maya Angelou tours Europe in *Porgy and Bess*. Guy stays in the US. Maya ends the tour and returns home when he is ill. She nurses her son back to health and promises never to leave him again.

1957   Maya Angelou's vocal music album, *Miss Calypso*, is released.

1958   Maya Angelou and Guy move to New York City. She becomes a member of the Harlem Writers Guild.

1960   After hearing Dr. Martin Luther King Jr. speak, Maya Angelou becomes the Northern coordinator for the Southern Christian Leadership Conference (SCLC). She writes and produces a fund-raising show, *Cabaret for Freedom*.
Maya marries African freedom fighter Vasumi Make. She moves her family to Cairo, Egypt, when her husband's life is threatened.
Maya becomes a journalist and writes and edits for the weekly newspaper *The Arab Observer*.

Maya Angelou performing in the Caribbean Calypso Festival, 1957.
Photo: Library of Congress

Maya Angelou in 1971 with *I Know Why the Caged Bird Sings*, the first volume of her bestselling memoir.
Photo: AP Images/stf

1961 Maya Angelou and her family move to Ghana. She continues her journalism work and writes for *The African Review* and *The Ghanaian Times*.

1963 Maya Angelou and Vasumi Make divorce. Maya meets Malcolm X, who is on his own sojourn, and he asks her to return to the United States and work with him at his new center. Maya discusses this with her son, who urges her to go on her own. Guy, in college, remains in Egypt.

1964 Maya Angelou returns to New York City to work at the Organization of African Unity. Malcolm X is assassinated on February 21.

1968 Dr. Martin Luther King Jr. is assassinated in Memphis, Tennessee, on April 4, Maya Angelou's birthday.

1969 The first volume of Maya Angelou's memoir, *I Know Why the Caged Bird Sings*, which details her difficult childhood, is published to critical acclaim.

1972 Maya Angelou writes the screenplay for the film *Georgia, Georgia*. She also composes the score. She is the first African American woman to have her script made into a film. It is nominated for a Pulitzer Prize.
Maya is nominated for a Pulitzer Prize for her book *Just Give Me a Cool Drink of Water 'fore I Diiie*.

1975 Maya Angelou is appointed to the Bicentennial Commission by President Gerald Ford to plan events to commemorate the 200th birthday of the United States in 1976.

1977 Maya Angelou appears in Alex Haley's television miniseries *Roots: The Saga of an American Family*.

1981 Maya Angelou joins the faculty at Wake Forest University and receives a lifetime appointment as Reynolds Professor of American Studies, where she is now addressed as Dr. Angelou.

1993 Dr. Angelou recites her poem "On the Pulse of Morning" at President Bill Clinton's first inauguration on January 20. The performance wins her a Grammy for Best Spoken Word or Non-Musical Album.

1995 Dr. Angelou wins a Grammy for Best Spoken Word or Non-Musical Album for her performance of her poem "Phenomenal Woman."
Dr. Angelou delivers her "Million Man March" message on October 16 at the Million Man March in Washington, DC.

Dr. Maya Angelou addressing the Million Man March from Capitol Hill on October 16, 1995.
Photo: AP Images/Doug Mills

1996 Dr. Angelou directs her first feature film, *Down in the Delta*. The film is released in 1998.

2002 Dr. Angelou wins a Grammy for Best Spoken Word Album for the audiobook of *A Song Flung Up to Heaven*, the sixth volume of her memoir.

2006-2010 Dr. Angelou hosts a radio show, "Ask Dr. Angelou," on Sirius XM Radio's *Oprah and Friends*.

2010 Dr. Angelou is awarded the Presidential Medal of Freedom by President Barack Obama. The ceremony takes place in 2011.

2013 Dr. Angelou's final volume of her memoir, *Mom & Me & Mom*, a tribute to her mother and grandmother, is published.

2014 Dr. Maya Angelou dies at her Wake Forest, North Carolina, home on May 28. Her funeral services are held at the Mount Zion Baptist Church in Winston-Salem and at the Wait Chapel on the grounds of Wake Forest University.

President Barack Obama awarding Dr. Maya Angelou the 2010 Presidential Medal of Freedom.
Photo: AP Images/Pablo Martinez Monsivais

Note from the Author

I wish I could share that the stigma and shame around child sexual abuse has diminished. It has not. Honoring the strength of unheard survivors, my favorite aunt included, as well as honoring Dr. Maya Angelou, a woman who I so strongly associate with forgiveness, joy, and deep belief, who found her healing in the written word, is what led me to capture Maya's life in verse form. Below are resources for those who may be affected or who wish to support someone affected by sexual violence.

Childhelp: childhelp.org

A twenty-four-hour, seven-days-a-week child-abuse hotline with professional counselors providing crisis intervention, information, literature, and referrals.

National Children's Alliance: nationalchildrensalliance.org

A nonprofit organization whose mission is to provide training, technical assistance, and networking opportunities to communities seeking to plan, establish, and improve child advocacy centers. The centers coordinate investigation and intervention services with professionals and agencies to create a team with a child-focused approach to sexual abuse cases.

Sexual Assault Awareness Month: nsvrc.org/saam

The month of April is Sexual Assault Awareness Month. This initiative aims to shine the light on sexual violence as a first step in raising awareness about the problem.

Stop It Now!: stopitnow.org

The Stop It Now! hotline provides resources for abusers and those at risk of abusing, helping them to stop the abuse and seek help. The helpline is available for abusers, for people at risk of abuse, and for their friends and family to call for information.

Selected Bibliography

Angelou, Maya. *The Collected Autobiographies of Maya Angelou*. New York: Modern Library, 2004.

———. *The Complete Collected Poems of Maya Angelou*. New York: Random House, 1994.

———. *I Know Why the Caged Bird Sings*. New York: Ballantine Books (mass market edition), 2015.

———. *On the Pulse of Morning*. New York: Random House, 1993.

———. *Phenomenal Woman: Four Poems Celebrating Women*. New York: Random House, 1995.

———. *Wouldn't Take Nothing for My Journey Now*. New York: Random House, 1993.

Dunbar, Paul Laurence. "Sympathy." In *The Complete Poems of Paul Laurence Dunbar*. New York: Dodd, Mead and Company, 1913.

Pettit, Jane. *Maya Angelou: Journey of the Heart*. New York: Puffin Books, 1998.

Schnall, Marianne. "An Interview with Maya Angelou." *Psychology Today*. https://www.psychologytoday.com/us/blog/the-guest-room/200902/interview-maya-angelou.

Quotation Sources

Back cover and pages 42–43: "Just like moons and like suns, . . .": from "Still I Rise" from *And Still I Rise: A Book of Poems* by Maya Angelou. Copyright © 1978 by Maya Angelou. Used by permission of Random House, an imprint and division of Penguin Random House LLC. All rights reserved.

page 6: "an unopened present": Maya Angelou. *I Know Why the Caged Bird Sings*, p. 16.

pages 16–17: "To be, or not to be . . .": William Shakespeare. *Hamlet, the Prince of Denmark* 3.1.56.

pages 18–19: "It was the best of times, . . .": Charles Dickens. *A Tale of Two Cities*.

pages 40–41: "A free bird leaps on . . .": from "Caged Bird" from *Shaker, Why Don't You Sing?* by Maya Angelou. Copyright © 1983 by Maya Angelou. Used by permission of Random House, an imprint and division of Penguin Random House LLC. All rights reserved.

page 44: "We may encounter many defeats . . .": Maya Angelou, in Schnall.